D0484331

NATIVE AMERICAN LEADERS
OF THE WILD WEST

SITTING BULL

❊Sioux Warrior❊

William R. Sanford

ENSLOW PUBLISHERS, INC.

Bloy St. & Ramsey Ave. P.O. Box 38
Box 777   Aldershot
Hillside, N.J. 07205   Hants GU12 6BP
U.S.A.   U.K.

Library of Congress Cataloging-in-Publication Data

Sanford, William R. (William Reynolds), 1927–
    Sitting Bull, Sioux warrior / William R. Sanford.
        p. cm. — (Native American leaders of the Wild West)
    Includes bibliographical references and index.
    ISBN 0-89490-514-7
        1. Sitting Bull, 1834?-1890--Juvenile literature. 2. Dakota
Indians—Biography—Juvenile literature. 3. Dakota Indians—
Kings and rulers—Juvenile literature. 4. Dakota Indians—
History—Juvenile literature. I. Title. II. Series: Sanford, William R. (William
Reynolds), 1927– Native American leaders of the Wild West.
E99.D1S614 1994
978.004'975'0092—dc20
[B]   93-42255
                                                                 CIP
                                                                  AC
Printed in the United States of America

10 9 8 7 6 5 4 3 2 1

Illustration Credits: National Archives, pp. 6, 22, 23, 25, 27, 29, 32, 33, 34;
William R. Sanford, pp. 10, 30, 35, 41; Smithsonian Institution, p. 18; South
Dakota State Historical Society, pp. 8, 14, 38.

Cover Illustration: Paul Daly

CONTENTS

AUTHOR'S NOTE

This book tells the true story of the Hunkpapa Sioux chief Sitting Bull. Many mistakenly believe that his fame rests on the Battle of the Little Bighorn. But his true fame comes from his leadership of the Plains Sioux over many years. Following Custer's defeat, the press hurried to print stories about Sitting Bull. Some were made up, but others were true. The events described in this book all really happened.

The white people needed Native American chiefs to sign their treaties. To make this happen they often pretended that one person led an entire tribe. Only rarely did tribes have one leader. Yet one chief did lead all the Plains Sioux. But he signed no treaties. This chief's name was Sitting Bull.

THE SUN DANCE

In June 1876 Sitting Bull prepared to keep a vow. Months before he had asked *Wakan Tanka*, the Great Holy, to watch over his people through the winter. In return for this he promised to sacrifice his blood and endure pain at the Sun Dance. He would give the Great Holy a scarlet blanket.

Sitting Bull knew the white soldiers were coming closer. He believed the slow and painful ritual would help insure victory for his people. Sitting Bull was forty-five years old. He knew what lay ahead, having endured the Sun Dance ritual before. He proudly wore the scars on his chest and back.

From the woods, warriors chose a cottonwood tree. It would serve as the symbol of the enemy. The warriors carried it to their camp. There they set it erect in a hole.

Priests painted the tree. The west side became red; the south, yellow; the east, green; and the north, blue. At the

At the Sun Dance, the Sioux sacrificed blood and endured pain. These formed offerings to Wakan Tanka, the Great Holy.

top they placed a red robe, bits of tobacco, and dried buffalo hide. The priests painted Sitting Bull's hands and feet red. Then they painted blue stripes across his shoulders to symbolize the sky.

It was now time to begin the Sun Dance. Sitting Bull strode to the sacred tree. He sat on the ground, his back rested against the tree trunk. In a singsong voice he began to pray. Jumping Bull, his adopted brother, carried a sharp knife in one hand. In the other he held a needle-pointed awl. Beginning at Sitting Bull's right wrist, he lifted a bit of skin with the point of the awl. With the knife he sliced it away. The bit of flesh was small—the size of a matchhead.

Sitting Bull did not change expression. He continued his wailing prayer. Both men ignored the blood. Jumping Bull made five rows of ten cuts in each arm. They spanned from wrist to shoulder. Blood covered both of Sitting Bull's arms and dripped from his fingers. Sitting Bull had promised the Great Holy a scarlet blanket. His blood was that blanket.

Sitting Bull rose and faced the sun. He pierced the skin on his chest with two sharp wooden skewers. They were attached by thongs to the tree. He began bobbing up and down on his toes. The weight of his body slowly began to tear free the skewers from his flesh. From time to time he looked into the sun. Sitting Bull prayed that the sun would protect his people. The rhythmic dance lasted all day and all night. During that time he did not eat or drink.

Sitting Bull was exhausted. At noon the next day, he staggered a few steps. The last skewer finally pulled loose, and he fell to the ground unconscious. As he slowly came to, Sitting Bull had a vision. He saw the soldiers of the white people's army. They were entering the Sioux camp, riding in defeat. Their heads were bent and their hats fell off. He heard a voice say, "I give you these because they have no ears."[1]

Sitting Bull told the Sioux what his dream meant. They would win a great victory. The whites would die in battle because they would not listen to sense. He added, "These soldiers are gifts of *Wakan Tanka*. Kill them, but do not take their guns or horses. Do not set your hearts upon the goods of the white man. It would prove a curse to this nation."[2]

The camp quickly packed. Sitting Bull knew the battle was coming soon.

Sitting Bull was both chief and holy man.

A BOY NAMED SLOW

The boy who would one day become Sitting Bull began his life during the winter of 1831. He was the first son born to Returns Again and his wife Mixed Days. They were Hunkpapas, a branch of the Plains Sioux. They lived in what is now South Dakota. The baby had no name at first. The Sioux believe that people must earn their names for themselves.

The small boy never hurried. He liked to grasp items in his small hands. He stared at the items with wide eyes and a serious face. His movements were clumsy. Thus the child gained the nickname *Hunkesi,* meaning "slow." But his mother denied that the boy was slow. She said that he was only cautious.

Years before, the Plains Sioux had lived in the eastern forests. Their enemies, the Chippewas, obtained guns from white traders. The Hunkpapas moved west across the northern Great Plains in pursuit of game. Huge herds of buffalo roamed the grasslands. Soon after moving there, the Sioux gained horses from Spanish settlers far to the south. Horses became central to their way of life. They made it easier for the Sioux to hunt and move from place to place. Raiding other tribes for horses became a part of Hunkpapa life.

The land where Slow grew up was harsh. Winter cold could quickly bring death. In summer the sun blazed, scorching the prairies yellow and brown. The Hunkpapas needed to be tough to survive.

The buffalo helped by providing most of what they

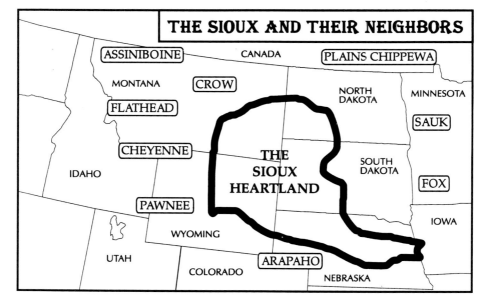

The Sioux were just one of many tribes living in the Great Plains. Since their territories overlapped, the tribes competed for the same resources. As a result, they often raided each other's camps.

needed. Its skin became robes and cover for their tipis. The Hunkpapas made cups and tools from the horns. They ground the hoofs to make glue. Buffalo sinews provided thread and bow strings. Sun-dried strips of buffalo meat became jerky, a food that lasted a long time without spoiling. Dried meat mixed with fat and berries became storable pemmican.

As a child Slow watched when Mixed Days helped break camp. First his mother took down the tipi. Then she loaded the folded skins and poles onto a travois. Two poles with cross branches formed these rough sleds. Returns Again's ponies dragged the travois behind them wherever his band moved its camp.

By the time he was eight, Slow had his own pony. He played at taking "coup." This involved touching an enemy, dead or alive, with a special stick. A warrior gained more honor by taking coup than by killing the enemy. Returns Again gave Slow a toy bow and arrow. The boy never tired of playing with them.

When he was fourteen Slow decided he was old enough to become a warrior. One summer night he learned that a war party was planning to raid the Crows. The next morning Slow mounted his pony and waited. He had no weapons. He carried a red coup stick. Slow announced to the warriors that he was coming too. They smiled at the idea. At last his father nodded his consent.

The Crows were just over the hill. A warrior gave a signal. Slow dug his heels into his pony. Armed only with the coup stick, he led the charge. A Crow warrior raised his bow. But before he could fire an arrow, Slow struck his arm with the coup stick. A Sioux riding behind Slow quickly killed the Crow. The other Crows soon fled, leaving behind their horses. This time the Sioux had won. The Crows would continue the fight another time.

Returns Again led the warriors on the way home. In the family tipi he painted Slow from head to foot in black. This was the color of victory. "My son is brave!" Returns Again chanted. From this day on his name will be *Tatanka Yotanka*, "Sitting Bull."[1]

THE YOUNG WARRIOR

The young warrior Sitting Bull learned the arts of war. He could string his bow in a flash. He could unleash his arrows with great force and he thought before acting. It was he who chose the best time for raiders to strike their foe.

Sitting Bull married Scarlet Woman. She was the first of his many wives. A year later she gave birth to a son. But that winter was bitterly cold. And before spring both his wife and baby had died.

Soon after this Sitting Bull joined a raiding party. They came upon a family of four from another tribe. The raiders killed the father, mother, and a small child. An eleven-year-old raised his toy bow and arrow to fight. When he saw Sitting Bull he cried, "Big Brother, help me!"[1] Sitting Bull spared his life. He took the boy back to the Hunkpapa camp. The chiefs allowed him to adopt the

As a young man, Sitting Bull earned respect for his bravery and courage. When his father was killed by Crows, he did the honorable thing and sought revenge.

child. When the boy grew up, he earned the name Kills Often.

Sitting Bull joined a warrior society. The Strong Hearts were brave men. They pledged never to retreat during a fight. They chose Sitting Bull to be the sash wearer. In battle he wore a long thin sash of red cloth. He staked the ends to the ground with a lance. He could not move from that spot until the fighting ended.

One day Sitting Bull was away hunting. Crows entered the Hunkpapa camp and killed Returns Again. When Sitting Bull returned, he organized a pursuit. Soon they caught up with the Crows. Sitting Bull spotted the man who had killed his father. The Crow fired, hitting Sitting Bull in the foot. With one blow of his lance, Sitting Bull knocked his foe from his horse. Sitting Bull drew his knife. He then killed the Crow, avenging his father's death. But Sitting Bull's wounded foot did not heal properly. For the rest of his life, he walked with a limp.

When he was a child, Sitting Bull had seen few whites. Only a few trappers and traders came to their land. The finding of gold in California changed all this. "Forty-niners" headed west in great numbers. Other miners headed northwest on the Oregon Trail. In 1851 the United States government invited the Great Plains tribes to a meeting. The tribes agreed to allow the whites free passage on the trails. They permitted the U.S. Army to build forts along the trails. In return, they would receive $50,000 a year for fifty years.

The Army built the forts quickly. Trouble soon followed. In 1854 a group of Brulé Sioux wiped out a patrol of thirty men. In revenge an army of 1,500 destroyed an unarmed band of Sioux under Little Thunder. His band was not the Sioux who had killed the soldiers. The white's policy was now clear. If any Sioux broke the peace, all Sioux would suffer.

The Santees were eastern or Dakota-speaking Sioux. They lived on a reservation in Minnesota. By the spring of 1862, the Civil War had delayed promised food for the tribe. So Chief Little Crow led attacks on settlers in the Minnesota Valley. In the fall the Army struck back. Many of the Dakota Sioux surrendered. The Army sent 1,300 Santees to a reservation on Crow Creek in the Dakotas. More than half died the first winter.

In the spring of 1864, Sitting Bull visited Crow Creek. What he saw sickened him. He resolved to fight the whites if they ever came to his country.

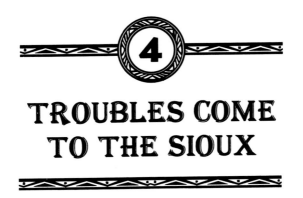

TROUBLES COME
TO THE SIOUX

In 1865 the U.S. Army began its war against Sitting Bull. For two months General Alfred Sully led his men across the northern plains. They did not see a single Hunkpapa. In August, United States government policy changed. A steamboat came up the Missouri River. It bore peace commissioners and presents for the Sioux.

Father Pierre Jean De Smet urged the Sioux to make peace. Sitting Bull stayed away. A few chiefs signed a treaty. The government acted as though all the chiefs had signed. The treaty allowed the building of forts and roads on Sioux lands. People in the east read the news. They thought the Bozeman Trail to the Montana goldfields was now safe.

Red Cloud, chief of the Oglala Sioux, led the fight against the use of the Bozeman Trail. For two years he attacked the forts along it. Captain William J. Fetterman once boasted he could ride through the Sioux Nation with just eighty men. But in December 1866 the Sioux wiped out his entire eighty-one-man unit.

The next year the Sioux gathered at Standing Rock. For the first time they would choose a chief to lead all Sioux. They picked Sitting Bull. Four chiefs came to his lodge. They escorted him to a ceremony. In turn, each chief smoked a pipe. They made speeches praising Sitting Bull. The chiefs gave Sitting Bull a white horse, a bow

At Standing Rock, the Sioux chose Sitting Bull as their leader. This later scene there shows Sitting Bull being accused of urging the Crows to go on the warpath.

with ten arrows, and a flintlock gun. They crowned him with a war bonnet. The eagle plumes draped to the ground. They told him, "Think always of *Wakan Tanka*, the one above. Second, you are to use all your powers to care for your people, and especially the poor."[1]

Father De Smet tried again to make peace in May 1868. He rode to meet with Sitting Bull. The chief told him, "I told [the whites] I did not want their [gifts], nor could I sell my country. My father lived and died here. So would I. And if our white brothers would do right, we would never have had war. I always liked to have goods to trade for. . . . I cannot bear the idea of having the country filled up with white men."[2]

Red Cloud came to a peace conference at Fort Laramie. He had won his demand that the forts and trails be closed. In November 1868 Red Cloud signed the treaty. It promised most of the Dakota Territory to the Sioux. The area covered all present-day South Dakota west of the Missouri River. The Black Hills were to belong to the Sioux for as long "as the grass shall grow and the waters shall flow."[3] Within this territory, agencies would serve all the Sioux bands. Whites were banned from this land forever. Sitting Bull had refused to attend or sign. The Hunkpapas were still free.

Sitting Bull had to defend his homeland against other tribes. The Crows came to steal his herds of horses. Sitting Bull led the fight that drove them away. He attacked the Flatheads to drive them from the buffalo country. In that battle an arrow pierced his forearm. A rumor went around that Sitting Bull was dead. But he had only fainted when friends pulled out the arrow.

Some people would later write that the great chief was only a medicine man, not a warrior. This is plainly false; he was both. By this time Sitting Bull had counted coup on sixty-three enemies.[4]

THE SIOUX VERSUS THE RAILROAD

The Union Pacific wanted to build a railroad across the Sioux lands. Army units guarded surveying parties. In 1872 Sitting Bull led attacks against them. During one fight Sitting Bull showed his contempt for his foe. Bravely he walked into the open ground between the two forces. He calmly sat on the ground and lit his pipe. He smoked a bowlful of tobacco while bullets whipped around him. When he finished, he walked unhurt out of rifle range.

A depression in 1873 briefly stopped the laying of track. The next year the Army planned to build a fort to guard the railway workers. The army sent troops to find a fort site. Their leader was Lieutenant Colonel George Armstrong Custer. Custer found traces of gold in the Black Hills.

The Fort Laramie treaty promised the Sioux that the Black Hills would be theirs forever. But press reports of the gold drew hundreds of miners. By 1875 over a

In 1874, Lt. Colonel George Armstrong Custer led a force into the Sioux's sacred Black Hills.

thousand prospectors camped in the Black Hills. The United States government offered to buy the land from the Sioux. Red Cloud offered to sell the Black Hills for $600,000,000. The government said they would pay $6,000,000. Neither side would budge. The next move was up to the government.

In November the government set a deadline. All Sioux were to be on their reservations by January 31, 1876. Those who did not would be considered hostile. They would be attacked and driven onto the reservations. The Sioux did not live by the white man's calendar. Such a deadline had no meaning to many of them. Sitting Bull ignored the demand.

In March 1876 General George Crook took to the field. He had ten companies of cavalry and two companies of infantry to back up his threat. He first attacked a

Dull Knife was a chief of the Cheyenne. His tribe answered Sitting Bull's call to arms.

Cheyenne camp on the Tongue River. The Cheyenne were hurrying across Sioux land to get to the reservation. The surviving Cheyenne joined Sitting Bull. He called a council. Sitting Bull's message was, "We must stand together or they will kill us separately. Those soldiers have come shooting. They want war. All right. We'll give it to them."[1]

Sitting Bull sent messengers to all bands of Sioux, Cheyenne, and Arapaho. They went to every camp on and off the reservation. They repeated Sitting Bull's words, "It is war. Come to my camp at the Big Bend of the Rosebud. Let's all get together and have one big fight with the soldiers."[2]

The word swept through the camps like a prairie fire. Many of the young men had tired of reservation life. They soon traded for the guns, powder, and bullets that they would need to fight. In June they took the trail for the Rosebud Creek. The grass was high enough to feed their ponies. Other bands sensed that they must fight now. If not, the Black Hills would be lost. They too came to Sitting Bull.

Army scouts kept an eye on the gathering of the Sioux. Three bluecoat armies headed for Sitting Bull's Rosebud camp. General Crook led over one thousand soldiers. They would come from the south. From the west came 450 men led by Colonel John Gibbon. General Alfred Terry led 925 men coming from the east. Among Terry's men was the Seventh Cavalry. It was led by "Yellowhair," Lieutenant Colonel Custer.

The Sioux knew that the armies were coming. Each day scouts brought back reports to the camp. They told Sitting Bull where the Pony Soldiers (cavalry) and Walk-a-Heaps (infantry) were. On June 9 the Sioux skirmished with Crook's men on the Tongue River. At the Rosebud camp, Sitting Bull completed his sacrifice during the Sun Dance. He predicted the Sioux would soon win a great victory.

In the Sun Dance, skewers through the flesh linked the dancer to a sacred tree.

THE LITTLE BIGHORN

Sitting Bull's Sun Dance vision would come true within a few days. The Sioux would win two big battles. On June 17, General George Crook led more than 1,300 soldiers to Rosebud Creek. Sitting Bull was still tired from his Sun Dance ordeal. Despite this he rode along with the Hunkpapas. Crazy Horse led the Sioux into the battle. Sitting Bull had warned them about the fast-firing guns of the soldiers. The Sioux must not dash forward to try to take coup.

Over a thousand braves attacked the soldiers. After five or six hours Crook pulled back. At this point the Sioux set fire to the prairie grass. They tried to drive off the soldiers' horses. The Sioux were willing to quit fighting. They had done what they came to do. Crook would not advance further. For the rest of the summer, Crook's forces camped where the hunting and fishing

In a Sun Dance vision, Sitting Bull foresaw a Sioux victory at the Little Bighorn.

were good. For now the Sioux camp on the Little Bighorn was safe from attack.

Sitting Bull knew this was not the battle he saw in his vision. No soldiers had fallen into the Sioux camp. The battle in the vision came about eight days later. Sitting Bull was with his family. In his tipi were two wives, sons, daughters, and newborn twins. His aged mother was nearby. Once a day the chiefs met in a council tipi. Sitting Bull was the old-man chief of all the tribes. His scouts told him Crook's men were still in retreat. The young warriors wanted to ride out to raid. Sitting Bull used his power to keep the tribes together. Then they could defend the camp if more soldiers came.

On June 25 scouts brought word. Soldiers were coming up the Little Bighorn from the south. Terry had ordered Custer to wait when he found the Sioux camp. Custer disobeyed and rode forward.

Sitting Bull armed himself with a .45 revolver. He carried his 1873 Winchester carbine. He began to round up the women and children. As medicine man and war chief, his job was to get them away from the battle. The Sioux thought that, at forty-five, he was too old to lead them in battle. He shouted to the young men to do something brave today.[1]

Major Marcus Reno led 150 men of the Seventh Cavalry. About 3 P.M., they attacked the southern edge of the Sioux camp. This was the Hunkpapa sector. Sitting Bull mounted his horse. He watched as Gall and a thousand warriors met Reno's attack. They killed or wounded half of Reno's men. Reno retreated across the river. Sitting Bull returned to the camp.

More soldiers appeared on a ridge across the stream. Custer led his 215 men toward the camp. Sitting Bull urged Gall's men to continue their fight. Crazy Horse would deal with the new threat. The Sioux appeared on all sides of the cavalry. Sitting Bull feared the soldiers would charge. The Sioux might then break and run. Instead the soldiers dismounted. Soon the battlefield faded into a cloud of dust. Sitting Bull knew how the battle would turn out. His vision had told him.

Thousands of warriors crawled up the gullies toward the hilltop. Nearer and nearer they came to the soldiers. They arched their arrows into the soldier's ranks without

Gall, a Hunkpapa warrior, led the fight that stopped Reno's attack on the Sioux camp on the Little Bighorn.

exposing themselves to rifle fire in return. The odds began to win out. In time the soldiers' guns fell silent. Not one man remained alive. Custer died of wounds to the head and chest. Despite Sitting Bull's warning, the Sioux stripped the soldiers' bodies of clothes and weapons. They took the Army saddles and horses.[2] Sitting Bull rode to the battlefield. He felt joy mixed with sadness. The Sioux women began their death songs.

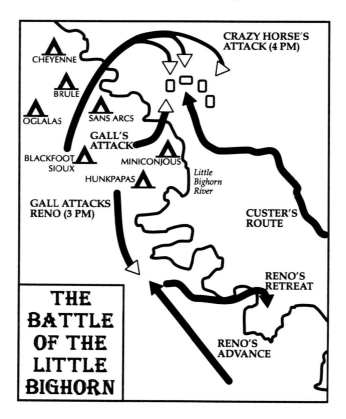

Though Sitting Bull was still leader of the Plains Sioux, Crazy Horse led the attack on the Seventh Cavalry.

FLIGHT TO CANADA

Two days later General Terry arrived at the Little Bighorn. His relief force found the vast camp empty. The Sioux had used up the local game and grass. Many of the Sioux thought they had won their fight. The Sioux did not understand. The white men were making war to the finish.

The bands split up. In this way they could hunt buffalo over a wide range. In September the soldiers caught up with a group of Sioux. At Slim Buttes, north of the Black Hills, General George Crook's men wiped out a Sioux village. Sitting Bull was thirty miles away. His relief force came too late. Some of the Sioux began to give up. Sitting Bull would not surrender.

A month later soldiers chasing him found a note. "I want to know what you are doing traveling on this road. You scare all the buffalo away. I want to hunt in this place.

General Crook led a force in pursuit of Sitting Bull. It moved slowly, due in part to the need for supplies to reach him by mules, such as the one shown here.

I want you to turn back from here. If you don't, I will fight you again. I want you to leave what you have got there and then turn back from there." It was signed, "I am your friend, Sitting Bull." At the end of the note was a postscript. "I mean all the rations you have got and some powder. I wish you would write as soon as you can."[1]

In October, Sitting Bull met General Nelson Miles under a flag of truce. Miles wrote, "He was a strong, sturdy looking man of about five feet eleven inches in height. [He was] well built, with strongly marked features, high cheek bones, prominent nose, straight thin lips, and a strong under jaw. . . . He was [a] man of few words."[2]

Neither side would give in. Sitting Bull would not go to a reservation. He told Miles all whites should leave the area. Miles gave Sitting Bull fifteen minutes to give in or face a battle. Sitting Bull raced to his village and called for a fight. The battle lasted two days. Sitting Bull retreated over forty miles. All winter long the soldiers harried the Sioux. Many Sioux gave up and moved to the reservation.

The Sioux called the Canadian border the "medicine line." They knew the soldiers could not chase them across it. In December three thousand Sioux crossed into the "Grandmother's land." (The Sioux gave this name to Canada, which was then ruled by Great Britain's Queen

The mass killing of buffalo by whites played a role in Sitting Bull's decision to meet with General Miles.

Victoria.) They settled around Wood Mountain in Saskatchewan. In May 1877 Sitting Bull joined them.

The Northwest Canadian Mounted Police laid down the rules. The Sioux could not steal horses or anything else. They could not fight with any other tribes. Above all they could not cross the border to hunt or raid. Sitting Bull promised that he and his young men would follow these rules. That summer Chief Joseph asked Sitting Bull to come to the aid of the Nez Percé. Sitting Bull had given his word not to recross the border. He sadly refused.

One rule was hard to keep. Few buffalo roamed the area. Sometimes the Sioux tried to slip across the border.

Sitting Bull's mother lived to see her son become a grandfather. Shown here are his mother, Sitting Bull, his daughter, and his grandson.

The Army chased them back. The Sioux grew hungry. The Canadians refused to send them food. "You are not Canadians," they said.

In small groups the Sioux left Sitting Bull. By 1881 only 185 remained; most were old. Sitting Bull led his band to Fort Buford, North Dakota, seventy miles south of the border. The Army had promised to send Sitting Bull to join the other Sioux. Instead they sent him to Fort Randall, South Dakota. They kept him as a prisoner of war for two years. At last in 1883, Sitting Bull joined the other Sioux at Standing Rock Agency, North Dakota.

Sitting Bull came to the Standing Rock Agency in the Dakota Territory in 1883. He lived here with his people for most of the 1880s.

SITTING BULL
GOES ON TOUR

In the fall of 1884 a showman, Alvaren Allen, asked Sitting Bull to go on tour. To persuade him Allen made a false promise. He said he would arrange for Sitting Bull to meet with President Garfield. Sitting Bull wanted to tell the President about his people's problems.

The tour visited fifteen cities. Ads for the show called Sitting Bull "the slayer of Custer." At each show the old chief waved and spoke to the crowds. But Sitting Bull's friendly greeting suffered in translation. The "interpreter" gave the crowd his own hair-raising account of the Battle of the Little Bighorn.

A fellow performer in the show, Annie Oakley, dazzled Sitting Bull. She shot cigarettes from her husband's mouth. And she drilled dimes held between his fingers. Since Annie was only five feet tall, Sitting Bull called her *Watanya Cicilia*. For once the interpreter reported his words correctly. They meant "Little Sure Shot." Annie's nickname stuck from then on. Sitting Bull "adopted" the sharpshooter as his daughter.

The next year Sitting Bull joined the show of Buffalo Bill Cody. He agreed to tour for four months. Nine other Hunkpapas went with him. Cody paid the chief fifty dollars a week. At that time working men earned one dollar for a twelve-hour day. Sitting Bull made sure his contract had one clause. He had the sole right to sell his autograph and photos.

Posters advertised the show. They claimed Sitting Bull had led the "massacre" at the Little Bighorn. They said he had personally scalped Custer. (Neither claim was true.) The tour opened in Buffalo, New York. Sitting Bull appeared in a full-feathered headdress. It reached the ground, even when he was standing. A beaded sash crossed his chest over a soft leather shirt. In the show Sitting Bull rode around the arena in a buggy. The crowds hissed and booed. The old chief could sense their hatred.

In Canada the audience was different. They did not jeer. They liked the fact that Sitting Bull had taken refuge in their country. They bought thousands of pictures of Sitting Bull and Cody. But, even in Canada, reporters asked Sitting Bull the same questions. They wanted to know about the Custer fight. He answered, "Nobody knows who killed Custer. Everybody fired at him. Custer was a brave warrior, but he made a mistake. The Indians honored him and did not scalp him. I fought for my

For many years afterward, the bones of horses killed in the fighting marked the site of the Battle of the Little Bighorn.

people. My people said I was right. I will answer for the dead of my people. Let the palefaces do the same."[1]

The cities awed Sitting Bull. He said, "I wish I had known this when I was a boy. The white people are so many.... If every Indian in the West killed one every step he took, the dead would not be missed among you. I go back to my people in one more moon. I will tell them what I have seen. They will never go on the warpath again."[2] When the tour ended Buffalo Bill gave Sitting Bull a parting gift. It was a gray circus pony, trained to do tricks.

Two years later Cody took his show to Europe. By royal command, they performed before Queen Victoria. Sitting Bull turned down a chance to go along. He would not meet the "grandmother" in whose country he took refuge. He said, "It is bad for me to parade around.... I am needed here. There is more talk of taking our land away from us."[3]

THE FINAL YEARS

His people did need Sitting Bull. Congress wanted to buy ten million acres of Sioux land. The United States government offered the tribe fifty cents an acre. This was a low price—even for that time! The government would then resell the land to whites for $1.25 an acre. In July 1888 the tribal leaders refused to sign.

The next year Congress offered $1.25 an acre. Each head of family was to keep 320 acres. The United States government would buy the rest. Land titles would remain in trust for twenty-five years. That way no one could cheat the Sioux out of their land. Despite Sitting Bull's objections, the deal went through. At once Congress cut the Sioux beef ration in half. Soon, ill-fed children died from measles, pneumonia, and tuberculosis.

In the fall of 1889 Kicking Bear brought news to Sitting

Bull. A great Native American prophet had appeared. Wovoka was a Paiute from Nevada. He claimed to have died and gone to the spirit world. There he met all his friends who had died before him. When he came back to life, he brought a message. Next spring all dead Native Americans would return to life. They would meet on a mountaintop with those who believed this prophecy. A flood would drown all whites. Then the buffalo would return. The Native Americans would live as they did before the whites came. To make this happen, they must dance the Ghost Dance.

On each reservation people danced. Each Ghost Dancer wore a special garment. A Ghost shirt was white, long, and loose. On it were paintings of the sun, moon, stars, and eagles. The dancers thought the shirt was bulletproof. They danced from mid-afternoon through the night. Many fainted. They claimed to see visions of the new world. Sitting Bull did not believe in the prophet. But he too danced to please those who did believe.

The new religion taught that no Native American should carry a weapon. The whites were worried. They asked about the Ghost Shirt. Weren't the "bulletproof" shirts proof of a coming uprising? At Standing Rock, schools and stores stood empty. No one worked on the farms. Everyone was dancing. The Indian Agent James McLaughlin told Sitting Bull to stop all Ghost Dancing. Sitting Bull gave the order. But, for once, his people did not obey.

McLaughlin wanted to arrest Sitting Bull and send him to prison. General Miles agreed. Before dawn on December 15, 1890, forty-three Indian police surrounded Sitting Bull's log cabin. Lieutenant Bull Head found Sitting Bull asleep on the cabin floor. "You are my prisoner," Bull Head said. "You must go to the agency." Sitting Bull agreed and put on his clothes.

The police and Sitting Bull left the cabin. Outside they found a crowd had gathered. Catch-the-Bear shouted,

The Ghost Dance religion spread to the Sioux by 1890. Sitting Bull's support for the religion was a factor in the decision leading to his arrest and death.

"You think you are going to take him. You shall not do it."[1] Catch-the-Bear fired his rifle, hitting Bull Head in the side. Bull Head's return shot struck Sitting Bull. A policeman, Red Tomahawk, fired at the same time. His shot hit Sitting Bull in the head. The great chief died instantly. Many felt the police had murdered him.

When the shots rang out, the old circus horse did as it was trained. It sat on its haunches and held out a hoof to shake hands. Then it ran away onto the plains. Soldiers took Sitting Bull's body to Fort Yates for burial. His tombstone reads:

SITTING BULL
Died Dec. 15, 1890
Chief of the Hunkpapa Sioux

Sitting Bull's followers joined the band of Chief Big Foot. The Miniconjou leader led his followers to Wounded Knee Creek, South Dakota. There troops of the Seventh Cavalry began to disarm them. When one Sioux resisted the troops opened fire. One count placed the Sioux dead at 300 (out of 350).[2]

That week marked more than the end of a year. It was the end of wars between whites and Native Americans. The fate of the Sioux fulfilled Sitting Bull's Sun Dance vision. Despite his warning the Sioux had taken the horses and guns of Custer's slain men. Now the Seventh Cavalry brought the Sioux destruction.

═NOTES BY CHAPTER═

Chapter 1

    1. Dorothy M. Johnson, *Warrior for a Lost Nation* (Philadelphia: The Westminster Press, 1966), p. 72.

    2. Benjamin Capps, *The Great Chiefs* (New York: Time-Life Books, 1975), p. 203.

Chapter 2

    1. Sheila Black, *Sitting Bull and the Battle of Little Bighorn* (Englewood Cliffs, N.J.: Silver Burdett, 1989), p. 14.

Chapter 3

    1. Sheila Black, *Sitting Bull and the Battle of Little Bighorn* (Englewood Cliffs, N.J.: Silver Burdett, 1989), p. 23.

Chapter 4

    1. Shannon Garst, *Sitting Bull: Champion of His People* (New York: Julian Messner, 1946), pp. 78–79.

    2. Stanley Vestal, *Sitting Bull: Champion of the Sioux* (Norman, Okla.: University of Oklahoma Press, 1957), p. 105.

    3. Sheila Black, *Sitting Bull and the Battle of Little Bighorn* (Englewood Cliffs, N.J.: Silver Burdett, 1989), p. 71.

    4. Dorothy M. Johnson, *Warrior for a Lost Nation* (Philadelphia: The Westminster Press, 1966), p. 61.

Chapter 5

    1. Stanley Vestal, *Sitting Bull: Champion of the Sioux* (Norman, Okla.: University of Oklahoma Press, 1957), p. 141.

    2. Ibid.

Chapter 6

1. Dorothy M. Johnson, *Warrior for a Lost Nation* (Philadelphia: The Westminster Press, 1966), p. 76.

2. Shannon Garst, *Sitting Bull: Champion of His People* (New York: Julian Messner, 1946), p. 131.

Chapter 7

1. Joseph Manzione, *I Am Looking to the North for My Life: Sitting Bull, 1876–1881* (Salt Lake City: University of Utah Press, 1991), p. 23.

2. Alexander B. Adams, *Sitting Bull: A Biography* (New York: G.P. Putnam's Sons, 1973), p. 331.

Chapter 8

1. Dorothy M. Johnson, *Warrior for a Lost Nation* (Philadelphia: The Westminster Press, 1966), p. 114.

2. Shannon Garst, *Sitting Bull: Champion of His People* (New York: Julian Messner, 1946), p. 158.

3. Johnson, p. 114.

Chapter 9

1. Dee Brown, *Bury My Heart at Wounded Knee* (New York: Holt, Rinehart, & Winston, 1970), p. 437.

2. Brown, p. 444.

GLOSSARY

awl—A sharp-pointed metal tool used for piercing.

band—A subdivision of a tribe, often only a few dozen in number.

chief—A leader of a band or tribe; often a chief was limited to a specific role such as leadership in war.

council—A meeting of the adults in a tribe; all warriors had the right to express their opinions.

coup—The gaining of prestige or status by a specific action; the Sioux took coup by touching an enemy in battle.

Ghost Dance—A ritual performed by Native Americans to prepare for the return of the buffalo and rebirth of the dead.

lodge—The home of the Sioux; lodges were made of hide stretched over many poles.

pemmican—A food prepared by mixing dried meat with fat and berries; it could be stored for long periods.

reservation—An area set aside by the government to be the permanent home of a group of Native Americans.

scouts—Skilled frontiersmen; scouts served as lookouts, read tracks, found trails, and located game.

Sun Dance—A ritual of Sioux warriors. The dance thanked the Great Spirit for past favors and insured a favorable future.

treaties—Agreements between two governments; treaties between Native Americans and whites often dealt with the sale of land.

tribe—A large group of Native Americans who speak a common language and live in the same area.

warrior—An adult Native American fighting man.

MORE GOOD READING ABOUT
▬▬▬▬SITTING BULL▬▬▬▬

Adams, Alexander B. *Sitting Bull: A Biography.* New York: G.P. Putnam's Sons, 1973.

Andrist, Ralph K. *The Long Death: The Last Days of the Plains Indians.* New York: Macmillan, 1964.

Black, Sheila. *Sitting Bull and the Battle of Little Bighorn.* Englewood Cliffs, N.J.: Silver Burdett, 1989.

Brown, Dee. *Bury My Heart at Wounded Knee.* New York: Holt Rinehart, & Winston, 1970.

Capps, Benjamin. *The Great Chiefs.* New York: Time-Life Books, 1975.

Garst, Shannon. *Sitting Bull: Champion of His People.* New York: Julian Messner, 1946.

Hook, Jason. *Sitting Bull and the Plains Indians.* New York: Bookwright Press, 1987.

Johnson, Dorothy M. *Warrior for a Lost Nation.* Philadelphia: The Westminster Press, 1966.

Knoop, Faith. *Sitting Bull: The Story of an American Indian.* Minneapolis: Dillon, 1974.

Manzione, Joseph. *I Am Looking North for My Life: Sitting Bull, 1876–1881.* Salt Lake City: University of Utah Press, 1991.

O'Conner, Richard. *Sitting Bull: War Chief of the Sioux.* New York: McGraw Hill, 1968.

Vestal, Stanley. *Sitting Bull: Champion of the Sioux.* Norman, Okla.: University of Oklahoma Press, 1957.

INDEX